JS

D0891091

FACES OF YOGA

uncomfortable photos of people in strange positions

By Jonah Sargent

ISBN 978-0-692-58967-0

Visit www.jonahsargent.com to see more of his works.

ACKNOWLEDGEMENTS

Grateful acknowledgement is made to the following for permission to photograph during classes: Danielle Jokinen of Minnesota Power Yoga, Mitchel Molloy, Sarah Rosemary Anagnostou and Erika Peterson. Thanks mom, dad, step mom and step dad. You're all great. Thanks for being wonderful.

Special thanks to my sister for showing me how to put my legs behind my head and roll down the staircase when I was a chubby 4th grader.

"Life has become immeasurably better since I have been forced to stop taking it seriously."

- HUNTER S THOMPSON

For Audrey Grace, I love you.

ABOUT THIS PROJECT

When I first started yoga I was constantly distracted by how I looked and felt during class. In the era of Instagram profiles devoted to sexy yoga models posing on beaches it's important to remember that we all look bad during yoga so we should immerse ourselves in it and forget the rest.

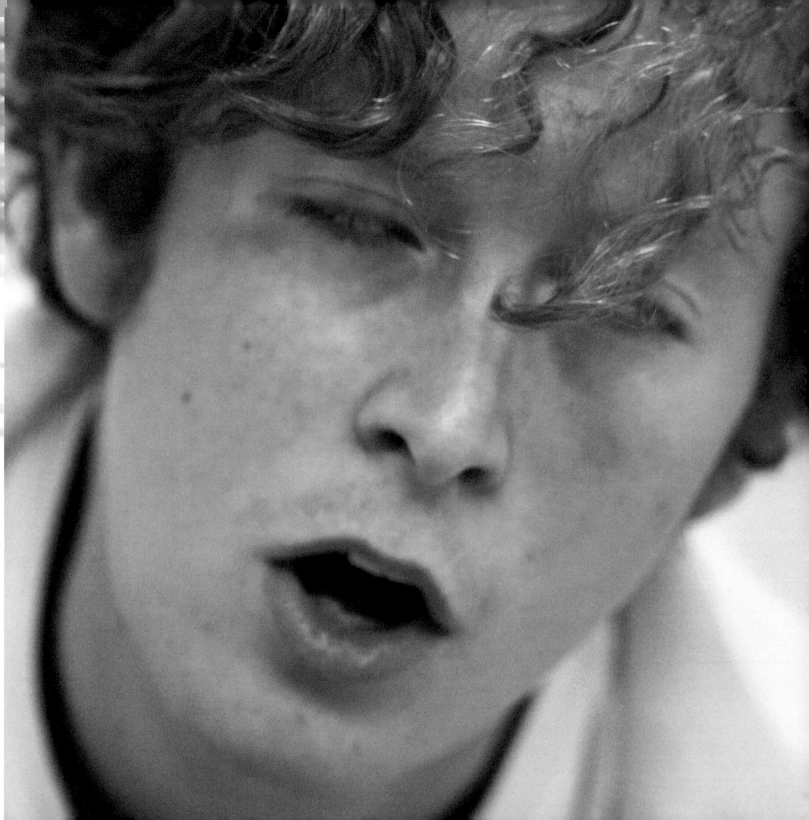

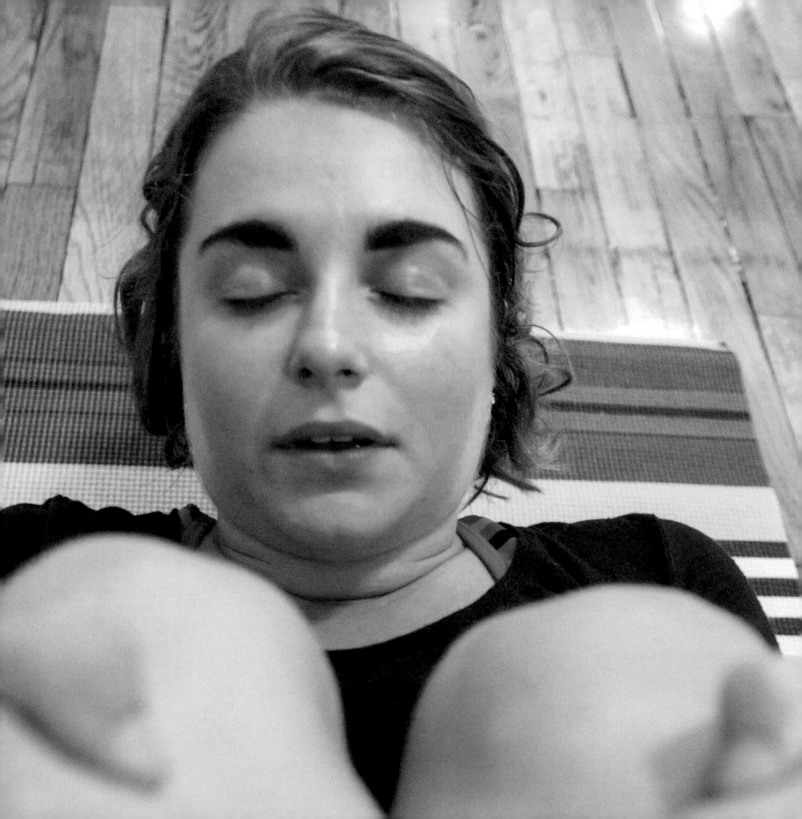

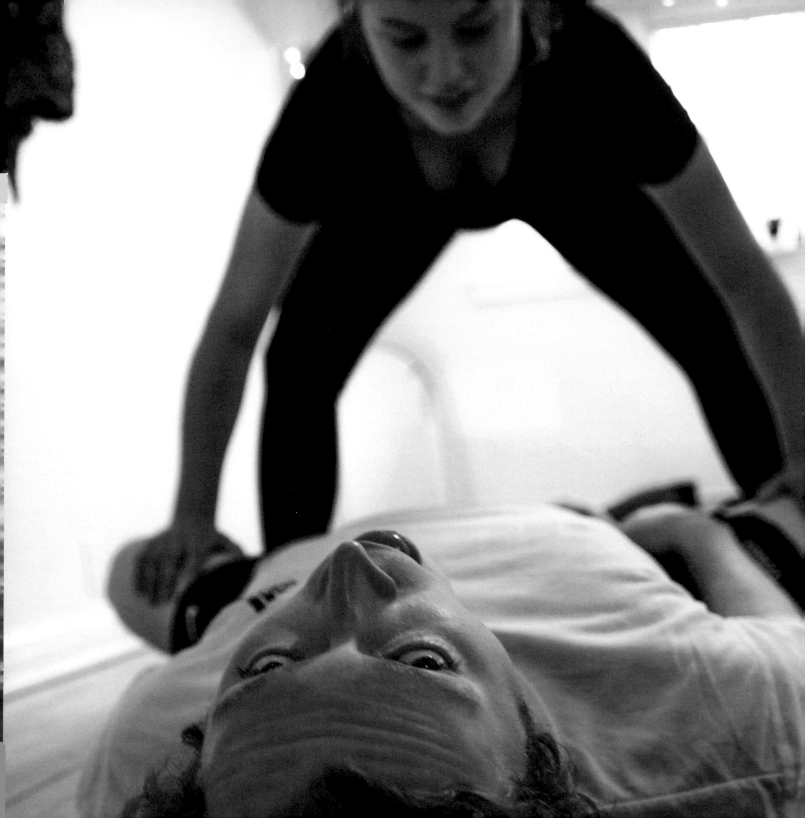

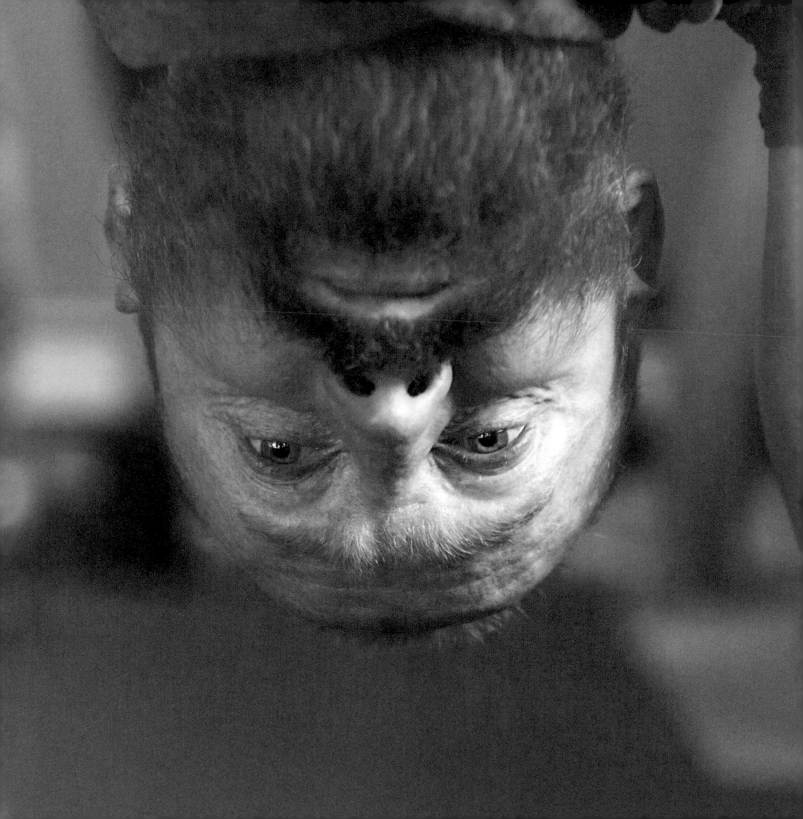

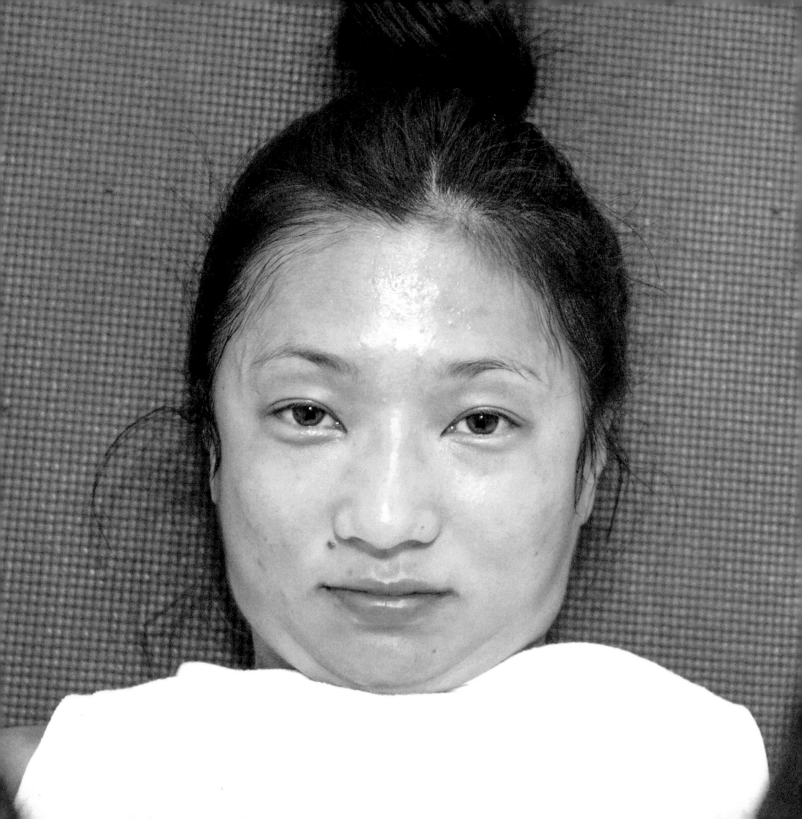

A SPECIAL THANKS TO ALL OF THE KICKSTARTER BACKERS

Cindy Paulson
Andrew Rollins
Jim Ell-Egermeier
Michelle Mallory Harma
Robert Sorensen
Julie Sit
Bonnie Gruen
Will Heegaard
Nesbitt Coburn
Andre Podleisek
Cole Hansen
Taylor Dunbar
Kalyn Cybulski
Heloise KjÃ¸lholm Rosing
Roger Heegaard
Sara Taksler
Kevin Boueri
Riley Curran
Magda Bilska
Nestor Bailly
Carrie Shanahan
Steve Nelms
David Castellano
Leah Frires
Alora Rando
Liza Burkin
Stephanie Engebretson
Patrick Risberg

Cally Johnsen
Melissa Faulkner
Stephanie Martin
Maggie Allexsaht
Pamela L'heureux
Seruni Putri Soewondo
Ariel Donahue
Andrew Grandbois
Thom Potts
Whitney Revoir
Rachel Seymour
Kevin O'Riordan
Meara Heaslip
Land Cook
Rachel Lustbader
Jesse LaVercombe
Zack Albun
Giovanna Conservani
Patrick Budde
Piotr Janetomski
Anastasia Anderson
Carlo Ferroni
Jeffrey Neal
Matthew Bolt
Kelsey Davison
Shaun Linnihan
Joshua Engebretson
Elizabeth Terry

Erin Freund
Ross Tatham
Julia Bogart
Emily Jo Cochrane
Kelly Beaudoin
Pa Dong Xiong
Marsha Maly
Danelle and Tim Reid
Karen Engebretson
Logan Quiggle
Matt A. Myers
Jamie Swezey
Defend Glendale
Lauren Jansen
Jordan Epstein
Alison McFall
Laura Rebecca
Kristin Conklin
Steve Herrington
Nir Ben-Shlomo
Christina Robohm
Alexander Rollins
Jon Igielnik
Laura Walker
Janie Trice
Melissa Paulson